ENERGETIC VIBRATING FREQUENCY

Books by Samuel K. Anderson

1. *God's Audacity: The Logic of God's Existence.*

2. *Whispers from My Mother.*

3. *Human's Audacity: The Leadership in Everyone.*

4. *The Kind Prince and Princess (Children's Book edition)*

5. *Finest Thickest P*****

6. *Energetic Vibrating Frequency*

7. *The* **CROWN** *of Fire*

ENERGETIC VIBRATING FREQUENCY

By

Samuel K. Anderson

Royal Publication
New Jersey, U.S.A

Energetic Vibrating Frequency

Energetic Vibrating Frequency

1st Edition 2020

ISBN-13: 978-1-7340066-3-6
Paperback Edition

Royal Publication

royalpublication@aol.com

Website: royalpublication.net

Energetic Vibrating Frequency

This book is fervently dedicated to my children:

Serenity, Samuel 2nd and Samuel 3rd.

Energetic Vibrating Frequency

Introduction

Energetic vibrating frequency is about discovering your true self through the energy within.

Everything you have been searching for to aid you to comprehend your being, your "why", your "how" and your "what" in light of your core of existence is found within you. You are the answers you seek.

Your spiritual, psychological, and physical health are all found within you. Let this book, Energetic Vibrating Frequency contribute to your journey and well-being. A 30-day energetic vibrating frequency journey that will open up portals connected to you since birth. This book is full of inter-dimensional wisdom, spirituality, energies, vibrations, and frequencies.

Energetic Vibrating Frequency

Table of Content

Rise 1: pg 13

Rise 2: pg 16

Rise 3: pg 19

Rise 4: pg 22

Rise 5: pg 25

Rise 6: pg 28

Rise 7: pg 31

Rise 8: pg 34

Rise 9: pg 37

Rise 10: pg 40

Rise 11: pg 43

Rise 12: pg 46

Rise 13: pg 49

Rise 14: pg 52

Rise 15: pg 55

Rise 16: pg 58

Rise 17: pg 61

Rise 18: pg 64

Rise 19: pg 67

Rise 20: pg 70

Rise 21: pg 73

Rise 22: pg 76

Rise 23: pg 79

Rise 24: pg 82

Rise 25: pg 85

Rise 26: pg 88

Rise 27: pg 91

Rise 28: pg 94

Rise 29: pg 97

Rise 30: 100

Rise 1

Envision your inner self embracing your core energy

-Samuel K. Anderson

Energetic Vibrating Frequency

Meditate on it. Summarize
your experience below:

Energetic Vibrating Frequency

Rise 2

Energetically vibrate your frequency through a state of balance, calm and internal security.

-Samuel K. Anderson

Energetic Vibrating Frequency

Meditate on it. Summarize
your experience below:

Energetic Vibrating Frequency

Rise 3

No creature, spirit, energy or power can steal your soul unless you allow it. Feel your soul. Be in tune with it.

-Samuel K. Anderson

Energetic Vibrating Frequency

Meditate on it. Summarize
your experience below:

Energetic Vibrating Frequency

Rise 4

Through blood and water, you are born into this material world. Through energy, spiritual vibration and individualized decision based frequency; you connect to the entire universe as one entity.

-Samuel K. Anderson

Energetic Vibrating Frequency

Meditate on it. Summarize your experience below:

Energetic Vibrating Frequency

Rise 5

Your body, consciousness and spirit can individually bring life or destruction to you. You ought to make sure that all three are in "perfect balance" for your ultimate sustenance.

-Samuel K. Anderson

Meditate on it. Summarize <u>your experience below:</u>

Energetic Vibrating Frequency

Rise 6

Imagine my day without you. You are my sunrise. My sunshine. My moonlight. I cannot imagine a second without you because you are the "me" I see in the mirror. Hello my spiritual sunshine, my spirit.

Hello my consciousness, my being.

Hello my earthly connection, my body. I am whole. I am free.

I am who I am.

~Samuel K. Anderson

Energetic Vibrating Frequency

Meditate on it. Summarize
your experience below:

Energetic Vibrating Frequency

Rise 7

Any Energy that doesn't Vibrate has no Frequency. I am the vibrating energetic frequency that rattles the cosmic realities of existence.

~Samuel K. Anderson

Meditate on it. Summarize
<u>your experience below:</u>

Energetic Vibrating Frequency

Rise 8

Life is a lesson within lessons sent to you by the universe to sharpen you with the ultimate purpose for you to attain your fullness as an eternal energy needed to complete the perfect stability of everything in existence.

~Samuel K. Anderson

Energetic Vibrating Frequency

Meditate on it. Summarize
your experience below:

Energetic Vibrating Frequency

Rise 9

Every blessing or curse is an outcome of your own actions or in-actions. You are consciously or unconsciously the product of everything that happens to you in this life.

-Samuel K. Anderson

Meditate on it. Summarize
your experience below:

Energetic Vibrating Frequency

Rise 10

The seity of your energetic vibrating frequency in your sanity, sanctity and spiritual etymological essence in direct connection to the absolute space in both existence and non-existence is intricately understood and communicated by none other but yourself.

~Samuel K. Anderson

Energetic Vibrating Frequency

Meditate on it. Summarize
your experience below:

Energetic Vibrating Frequency

Rise 11

The only time people ever become a liability financially, spiritually, physically, morally, socially and psychologically is when they give up on themselves.

~Samuel K. Anderson

Energetic Vibrating Frequency

Meditate on it. Summarize
your experience below:

Energetic Vibrating Frequency

Rise 12

Develop yourself into something terrific. Start your transformation now. Become the exact person you desire to become.

~Samuel K. Anderson

Energetic Vibrating Frequency

Meditate on it. Summarize
your experience below:

Energetic Vibrating Frequency

Rise 13

Do you ever wonder what the link that connects energy, vibration and frequency is? Well, you are the link. Yes you are that link that connects it all.

~Samuel K. Anderson

Meditate on it. Summarize
<u>your experience below:</u>

Energetic Vibrating Frequency

Rise 14

Everyone seems to be looking for a guru. This feeling of wanting or needing a guru, an expert or a supernatural connection is normal for everyone. However, many fail to realize that we are our own gurus. Yes, you are your guru. Your guru is in you. You were born with it. Tap into yourself to awaken your guru. Your guru is your soul, spirit, and consciousness. Let your energy vibrate the right frequency needed to awaken your guru.

~Samuel K. Anderson

Energetic Vibrating Frequency

Meditate on it. Summarize
your experience below:

Energetic Vibrating Frequency

Rise 15

Be peaceful, be calm, be in balance with the energies vibrating through you. The frequency of your internal energy has been communicating with you to choose what's right. The outer energies may sometimes distract you. Are you listening to that internal energetic vibrating frequency that aims at bringing you all the completeness you seek.

~Samuel K. Anderson

Energetic Vibrating Frequency

Meditate on it. Summarize
your experience below:

Energetic Vibrating Frequency

Rise 16

Starting today, your energetic vibrating frequency will flow through you like an eternal fountain of youthful water. Everything in and around you is at peace and in alignment with your energetic vibrating frequency.

~Samuel K. Anderson

Energetic Vibrating Frequency

Meditate on it. Summarize
your experience below:

Energetic Vibrating Frequency

Rise 17

When you finally connect with your energetic vibrating frequency you will understand why you have been out of balance in almost every situation including your physical, psychological and spiritual energies.

~Samuel K. Anderson

Energetic Vibrating Frequency

Meditate on it. Summarize
your experience below:

Energetic Vibrating Frequency

Rise 18

Your journey through your energetic vibrating frequency may be slightly hobbledehoy. Whether you have passed through that hobbledehoy state, currently going through it, or about to go through your hobbledehoy state; what matter most is your consistent focus of calmness through this journey.

~Samuel K. Anderson

Energetic Vibrating Frequency

Meditate on it. Summarize
your experience below:

Energetic Vibrating Frequency

Rise 19

Your psyche is the door through which your spiritual liberation initiates. Igniting this initiation gives you unbreakable wings to soar through great heights in both the material and immaterial realms.

-Samuel K. Anderson

Energetic Vibrating Frequency

Meditate on it. Summarize your experience below:

Energetic Vibrating Frequency

Rise 20

With the energetic power of "I AM" you become whomever you choose to become in a direct vibrational frequency transformation.

~Samuel K. Anderson

Energetic Vibrating Frequency

Meditate on it. Summarize your experience below:

Energetic Vibrating Frequency

Rise 21

You are full of inter-dimensional wisdom, spirituality, energies, vibrations, and frequencies bottled up within you. It's about time you let these supernatural energies flow within you. Focus, feel them within.

-Samuel K. Anderson

Meditate on it. Summarize your experience below:

Energetic Vibrating Frequency

Rise 22

You believe, so you become.
You are, so you exist. You
think, so you create. You
look inside yourself, so you
connect with your true self.
You embrace your true self,
so you are spiritual. Your
spirit is connected to your
energy. Your energy
vibrates in its own
frequency pathways
connecting you to all the
dimensions you choose to
enter.

~Samuel K. Anderson

Energetic Vibrating Frequency

Meditate on it. Summarize
your experience below:

Energetic Vibrating Frequency

Rise 23

Sometimes for you to see, feel and hear the energies hidden within earth and in the galaxies; you ought to close your physical eyes and turn on your internal faucet. There are energy portals all around us and if you listen closely, you will hear, feel and see these portals that can transport you into different dimensions.

~Samuel K. Anderson

Energetic Vibrating Frequency

Meditate on it. Summarize your experience below:

Energetic Vibrating Frequency

Rise 24

Exercise intellectual intelligence, emotional intelligence, conflict resolution, motivating yourself and others, verbal and non-verbal communication prowess, strategic and analytical thinking, action and service orientation, coaching yourself and others, plan, organize and execute without fear of favor. Finally, use wisdom to manage changes in diverse energies, vibrations and frequencies around you.

~Samuel K. Anderson

Energetic Vibrating Frequency

Meditate on it. Summarize
your experience below:

Energetic Vibrating Frequency

Rise 25

Why earth? What is your mission? Who sent you? Was it your WILL? Was it your choice? How do you have to accomplish your mission? What happens if you fail? What happens if you succeed? Where do you go after here? Do you end? Simple answer, you are here because you chose to be here. Your life is spiritual energy; hence, you do not end. You are eternal.

~Samuel K. Anderson

Energetic Vibrating Frequency

Meditate on it. Summarize <u>your experience below:</u>

Energetic Vibrating Frequency

Rise 26

To be in equitable alignment with nature you ought to be your own nature. Nature is your extension. Cast away all unnatural things to embrace all the natural things nature possess. That is you. You are a complete nature waiting to be explored by you.

~Samuel K. Anderson

Energetic Vibrating Frequency

Meditate on it. Summarize
your experience below:

Energetic Vibrating Frequency

Rise 27

I am everything.

So, who are you?

Who do you think you are?

Use the key of "I AM EVERYTHING I choose to be" to answer these questions. In that, you are indeed everything.

~Samuel K. Anderson

Energetic Vibrating Frequency

Meditate on it. Summarize <u>your experience below:</u>

Energetic Vibrating Frequency

Rise 28

Raise your frequency.

Raise your vibration.

Raise your energy.

Feel the serenity within you. Your energetic vibrating frequency is at its peak. Let it rise. Let it rise. Let it rise!!!

~Samuel K. Anderson

Energetic Vibrating Frequency

Meditate on it. Summarize your experience below:

Energetic Vibrating Frequency

Rise 29

Spirituality is the absolute frequency that vibrates your energy. (This definition is from my book "God's Audacity: The Logic of God's Existence"). **Your energetic vibration frequency is your absolute spirituality.**

~Samuel K. Anderson

Energetic Vibrating Frequency

Meditate on it. Summarize
your experience below:

Energetic Vibrating Frequency

Rise 30

Do you hear the universe calling? Listen. Be calm. Shut every material distractions down and listen. Just listen deeply and closely. The universe has been calling. The soles of your feet connects its feminine side of energy as your hair stretches to its masculine side of energy. You have always been at the heart of the universe.

Now, do you hear the universe calling? Your energetic vibrating frequency always needs to be high in order to get a clear connection with the universe. Can you hear it? The energy of the universe is pure. Can you feel it? Absorb the universe. Soak in its frequency. Vibrate with its vibrations. You are now one with the universe's energetic vibrating frequency.

~Samuel K. Anderson

Meditate on it. Summarize your experience below:

Energetic Vibrating Frequency

Energetic Vibrating Frequency

The

END

Energetic Vibrating Frequency

<u>Write down Your Reflections</u>

Energetic Vibrating Frequency

Energetic Vibrating Frequency

Samuel K. Anderson (BSBA, MBA, University of The Incarnate Word) is a Ghanaian American citizen and a member of the largest leadership honor society in the nation (United States of America) known as NSLS, The National Society of Leadership and Success. He has served as an astute leader, motivator, philanthropist, father, entrepreneur, mentor, wisdom seeker and educator.

He is a vibrant CEO and founder of two companies. A motivational and life coach speaker. He served in his early formal education years as the Regional Trustee for the Eastern Regional Students' Representative Council with the Council's aim to Emancipate Students through Dialogue and a Philosophy of Non-Violence, President of an NGO that aimed at educating the youths on drug abuse, Counselor, Director of Children's Ministry, and a School Teacher. He completed formal bible training education, enrolled at Seminary School for a while and also studied Theology at Central University College before transitioning to San Antonio College then transferred to University of The Incarnate Word to pursue bachelor's degree in Accounting and an MBA graduate level degree with concentration in Asset Management (Real Estate and Finance).

Kindly contact me: **samuelkanderson777@outlook.com** with your specific requirements for speaking events.